YORKSHIRE DALES

Halswood

Published by Halswood Stationers

Copyright © Halswood Stationers
Image copyright © John Morrison

British Library Cataloguing-in-Publication Data
A CIP record for this title is available
from the British Library

ISBN 978 0 85717 010 1

HALSWOOD STATIONERS
Halsgrove House,
Ryelands Industrial Estate,
Bagley Road, Wellington, Somerset TA21 9PZ
Tel: 01823 653777   Fax: 01823 216796
email: sales@halsgrove.com

Part of the Halsgrove group of companies
Information on all Halsgrove titles is available at:
www.halsgrove.com

Printed and bound in China by
Toppan Leefung Printing Ltd (010)

Front cover: Upper Swaledale, with the flank of
Kisdon Hill rising to the left.

Back cover: Arkengarthdale.

Title page: Morning mist begins to lift, uncovering the
flanks of Kisdon Hill in Upper Swaledale.

Right: Late-afternoon sun imparts a warm glow
to the stonework of a farmhouse in Burtersett,
Wensleydale.

Overleaf: From a nearby fell, Burnsall looks the
archetypal Dales village: a handsome church flanked
by old stone houses.

YOUR ADDRESS BOOK

The Yorkshire Dales National Park was created back in 1954. More than half a century later, we can be thankful that 680 square miles (1773 sq km) of glorious landscape remain unencumbered by motorways, theme parks and industrial estates.

It's an intimate landscape, hilly rather than mountainous. It's a managed landscape too, not the wilderness that some visitors imagine. The hand of man is visible at every turn. When the Dales were being enclosed, many voices were raised in protest. Ironically, most of them objected to the change of land use on aesthetic grounds. This unique landscape would be changed forever, they complained, if the Dales were to be parcelled up into walled fields. And now, a mere 150-200 years after most of the walls in the Dales were built, we can hardly imagine this landscape without the familiar drystone walls and fields and field-barns.

But the landscape of the Yorkshire Dales is seldom as placid or benign as the tourist brochures would suggest. The sky isn't always blue. And, every winter still, isolated Dales communities get cut off by snow.

Master-photographer John Morrison loves the light at dawn and dusk, rather than the bland, blue-tinged light in the middle of the day. He loves the drama that can occur when two weather fronts collide and doesn't feel that he has had a proper day's photography until he has been soaked twice! His sense of place and the excitement as well as the beauty of each scene, is evident again and again in the superb images reproduced here.

Address books tend to be well used and have a long life. Along with important contact details, they keep track of the user's friends and acquaintances, tracing their lives over time and from place to place. And, if properly attended to, an address book eventually becomes a journal in itself, and an attractive and permanent keepsake. Whether bought as a gift or for personal use, this Yorkshire Dales Address Book, with its superb pictorial reminders of the national park, will provide years of pleasure.

USEFUL ADDRESSES AND TELEPHONE NUMBERS

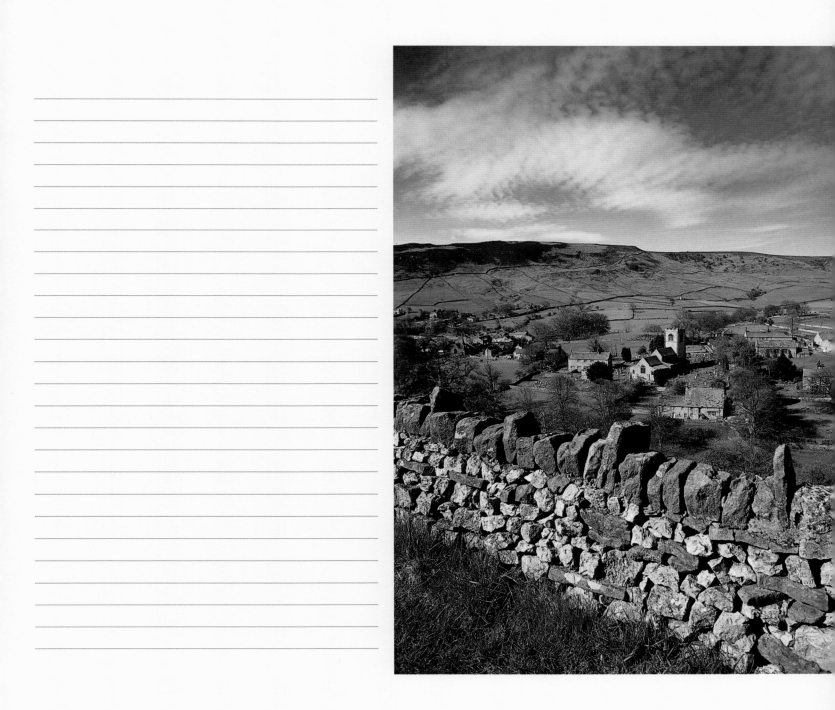

The mist creates a simple composition of wall, fence, barns, farmhouse,
road, tree, sheep and – in the background – the flanks of Pen-y-Ghent.

A

B

Ramsgill in Nidderdale: one of those delightful Dales communities
of sturdy stone cottages, which still retains its village green.

B

B

B

The church rises head-and-shoulders above the houses of Muker,
one of the most characterful villages of Upper Swaledale.

C

A dull autumn day in Arkengarthdale seems to accentuate the
colour of the foliage, as though the leaves were lit from within.

C

C

C

For centuries the economy of the northern Dales relied more on lead-mining than agriculture. Arkengarthdale, for example, is pocked-marked with spoil-heaps.

D

Darnbrook Farm, sheltered in its own tiny valley on the road between Malham Tarn and Arncliffe, now belongs to the National Trust.

D

D

D

Farms near Hawes in Wensleydale: dusted
with frost and cast in a warm evening light.

E

An obliging mallard maintains the symmetry at
Semer Water, the largest natural lake in the Dales.

E

E

E

The Norber Erratics near Clapham are boulders of Silurian slate,
left high and dry on pedestals of limestone by glacial action.

F

Small fields of irregular shape are generally some of the oldest enclosures in the Dales. Here they surround neighbouring farms in Arkengarthdale.

F

F

F

A profusion of garden flowers also adds colour to this
scene in the village of Burnsall in Wharfedale.

G

Back in 1657 they built houses to last many lifetimes; this
stone cottage is in the Wharfedale village of Conistone.

G

G

G

High summer near Grassington in Wharfedale, with knuckles of limestone pushing up through the sheep-cropped grass.

The flood plain of the River Swale, beneath the village of Gunnerside in Swaledale, is laid out with an intriguing pattern of barns and walls.

H

H

H

The broad valley of Wensleydale.

Ribblehead Viaduct, carrying the Settle–Carlisle
Railway over some of the Dales' most barren
terrain, with Whernside in the background.

I

J

East Gill Force, tumbling prettily over a rocky ledge, is
one of many waterfalls near Keld in Upper Swaledale.

J

A view of Swaledale – from the river in the valley bottom to the rough moorland and lead-mining spoil-heaps on the fells.

K

Trees protect a farmhouse from the worst of Pennine weather;
the valley beyond is Swaledale and the village, Low Row.

K

L

One of the most photographed views in the Dales: Upper
Swaledale, with the flank of Kisdon Hill rising to the left.

L

L

L

While some villages of the Dales are cramped, in others – such as Low Row in Swaledale – the farms and houses seem to keep their distance.

Early summer in Littondale – sunlit fields backked up by limestone scars.

M

M

M

Limestone pavements are very photogenic, as are the stunted, tenacious
trees that grow on them. This one is in Wharfedale near Conistone.

A favourite view in the Dales, from Crackpot Hall in Swaledale.

N

Limestone scenery, typical of the southern Dales;
this is Winskill Stones, not far from Settle.

O

o

The overhanging limestone cliff of Kilnsey Crag is
one of the best-loved landmarks in Wharfedale.

O

In evening light the pastures of Oxnop Gill in Swaledale look as though they've been returfed with green velour.

The evocative ruins of Bolton Priory: framed by
branches and viewed from across the River Wharfe.

PQ

Mist creates a fantasy landscape near Hawes,
with Ingleborough just visible in the distance.

Another view of Winskill Stones above the market
town of Settle, beneath a light covering of snow.

R

A roofscape of Settle, seen from the limestone cliff of Castleberg, as storm clouds approach.

Evening light picks out the Georgian façades of the houses on the cobbled street of Frenchgate, leading down to Richmond's Market Place.

S

S

S

The River Swale from lonely Crackpot Hall.

Wensleydale walkers enjoying a new fall of snow, with Hawes —
and its distinctive, lopsided church tower — in the background.

T

The Old Grammar School in Burnsall: a gift to the village from
Sir William Craven, Wharfedale's very own Dick Whittington.

_____

_____

_____

_____

_____

_____

_____

_____

_____

_____

_____

_____

Morning mist gives this upland scene in Swaledale
the rather theatrical look of a painted backcloth.

UV

Soft evening light picks out a cottage in Burtersett, Wensleydale.

W

A tractor provides a focus for this shot of
Pen-y-Ghent rising up through the mist.

W

A spot of colour, however small, draws the eye towards it. This red-roofed barn is in Oxnop Gill, Swaledale.

A peaceful scene near Malham: sunshine and shadows, sheep
grazing and a meandering path defined by limestone walls.

XYZ